6 Ways
We Encounter God

6 Decisions
That Will Change Your Life

Participant Workbook
DVD
Leader Guide

6 Things
We Should Know About God

Participant Workbook
DVD
Leader Guide

6 Ways
We Encounter God

Participant Workbook
DVD
Leader Guide

6 Ways

We Encounter God

Participant Workbook

Tom Berlin

with Karen Berlin

Abingdon Press
Nashville

Six Ways We Encounter God
Participant Workbook

Tom Berlin with Karen Berlin

Copyright © 2014 by Abingdon Press
All rights reserved.

This book is printed on acid-free, elemental chlorine-free paper.

ISBN 978-1-426-79468-1

14 15 16 17 18 19 20 21 22 23—10 9 8 7 6 5 4 3 2 1
MANUFACTURED IN THE UNITED STATES OF AMERICA

With God's help, I will draw closer to Christ through this six-week study as I commit to read the Bible and prayerfully reflect on its meaning for my life.

_____

My Name

_____

Start Date

Contents

Welcome!

We're glad you are participating in *Six Ways We Encounter God*. When you commit yourself to this six-week journey, we believe you will grow deeper in your relationship with Christ. You will gain the most from this study if you make the following practices a part of your journey:

1. **Attend a small group.** Your church offers small group opportunities where spiritual transformation can be encouraged and enhanced through community. Those gathered will have the opportunity to share and discuss their insights, questions, and life experiences and, most importantly, to apply lessons learned about their personal and corporate study. The study includes, in addition to this Participant Workbook, a DVD and Leader Guide to enhance learning and group involvement. We encourage all to join a small group for this study.

2. **Use the Participant Workbook five days a week.** This book is intended to draw you into a daily conversation with God by guiding you in reading key Scripture passages, responding to reflective questions, and journaling your thoughts about how this encounter applies to your life.

3. **Attend worship.** Our conversation with God is incomplete if we don't participate in individual and corporate worship. Go to church every week, but during the study make a special point of attending.

How to Use This Book

When you use this book each day, begin your time with prayer. Read the Bible passages assigned for the day. Answer the questions provided, journal on your own, or do a combination of these two options.

Write out a Scripture verse that speaks to you from the assigned reading. It may be a verse of encouragement, instruction, confession, or insight.

Observe what the verse says, and write a few sentences about its relevance to your life.

Relate the text to your life by applying it to a specific issue you are considering, a problem you are facing, or an encouragement God wants you to hear. Write a short paragraph in which you share what you are hearing from God's Word.

Decide to share with God the desire of your heart. As a result of reading this text, what do you want to do and who do you want to become? Share your thoughts by writing a short prayer to conclude your conversation with God.

God's Majesty and My Reverence

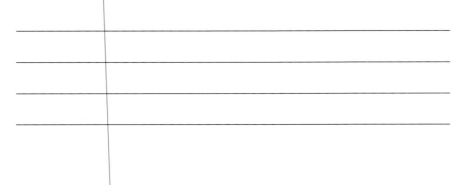

Day 1

Today's Scripture
Genesis 1:1–2:3; Psalm 104

Key Verse

How many are your works, LORD! In wisdom you made them all; the earth is full of your creatures.

Psalm 104:24 NIV

1. Describe a time when the majesty of God's creation inspired awe and reverence in you.

_____

_____

_____

_____

2. The author of Psalm 104 writes, "I will sing to the LORD all my life; I will sing praise to my God as long as I live." What inspires the psalmist to share such words of praise?

_____

_____

_____

_____

14

Going Deeper

Psalm 104 is a poetic retelling of the Creation story, praising God for the power and creativity displayed in the creation of the world. It is a love song for our Creator, as the author points out all the things he sees in the world and what they mean to him. The psalmist is amazed at the forethought God put into the world. The Creation story isn't just a list of things God made, it also shows the careful crafting that God put into every aspect of the world, including each and every human.

The other thing that's interesting about Psalm 104 is that it changes from past to present tense. The psalmist is reminding us that God didn't stop creating after that first week. God is still working in the world, caring for its creatures, cultivating its mountains and pastures, and astounding us with its beauty. God still wants us to look at creation, perhaps to see that the beauty we find there is a reflection of the nature of its Creator. We just need to stop and take the time to look.

> **Trivia Tidbit**
>
> *According to* Fausset's Bible Dictionary, *"leviathan" is a word used to describe both mythological sea dragons representing the chaos of creation (as in Psalm 74:14) and real water creatures like crocodiles (as in Job 41:1).*

Going Deeper Questions

3. What parts of creation cause you to recognize God's fingerprints in our world?

_____

_____

_____

4. When was the last time you took time to praise God for what you see there?

_____

_____

_____

5. What caused you to do this?

_____

_____

_____

6. How have you felt God shaping and creating something new in your life?

_____

_____

_____

Today's Scripture
Exodus14:1-31; Exodus 15:19-21; Psalm 29

Key Verse

And when the Israelites saw the mighty hand of the LORD displayed against the Egyptians, the people feared the LORD and put their trust in him and in Moses his servant.

Exodus 14:31 NIV

1. Why do the people doubt God's provision in the desert?

_____

_____

_____

_____

2. What does the word "fear" mean in Exodus 14:31?

respect, awe, wonder

_____

_____

_____

Going Deeper

There's a story about a schoolteacher and a young student who were talking about Israel's escape from Egypt. The teacher said that there are some parts of the Red Sea that are only a foot deep in the dry season, so the fact that Israelites got across it was no great miracle at all. But the child replied, "In that case, it's even more of a miracle, 'cause that means God stopped all of Pharaoh's army in only a foot of water!"

As modern people, we feel like we need to have all the answers to all the questions. We want to understand how everything works. But God has power over the things that we can't control and can't figure out. Our task is to be reverent enough to follow God's calling and do God's will. The miracle of parting the waters of the Red Sea was not so miraculous to God.

> ### Trivia Tidbit
>
> *An "Eastern wind" is shown throughout the Bible as a hot, strong, withering wind that dries up the Red Sea (Exodus 14:21), brings the plague of locusts to Egypt (Exodus 10:13), and torments Jonah for his ungratefulness (Jonah 4:8).*

Even in the face of such a powerful act, the Israelites had to decide whether to go back to Egypt or to step out and walk across the dry land. It would seem easy to trust God in such a moment, but it also would have been easy to get distracted by the walls of water all around. Sometimes the difficulties of our lives are just like that water. We can't hold them back with our own strength. Things slip through the cracks, and it doesn't matter if it's a foot of water or a mile—it's still going to make a mess. The key is to trust God in such times, and to walk with the Lord through the uncertainty as the children of Israel did. Only when we trust can God's majesty change our circumstances.

Going Deeper Questions

3. Where in your life is God calling you to step away from what is comfortable and into something that will force you to trust more?

DC, seminary, camp

4. Have there been times in your life when you've trusted in God? Write down what such times have taught you about God's character.

Day 3

1. What does Exodus 19 teach us about God?

_____

_____

_____

_____

_____

2. What does it teach us about people?

_____

_____

_____

_____

_____

Going Deeper

The holiness of God can be hard to grasp. When the people of Israel came to meet God at Mount Sinai, they were no more perfect than we are. They had been wandering in the desert for three months, complaining about the food and the water, fighting off enemies, and dealing with the heat while camping. They were probably dirty and stinky and not in a good mood. Yet God planned to come down and meet them.

For such an amazing guest, the people had to prepare. They had to purify themselves, wash their clothes, and avoid anything that would make them impure or dirty. Why? Because the dirt on their bodies was a symbol of the sins that they carried with them—their grumbling, fighting, and lack of trust. This ritual cleaning was a way to become symbolically clean, to accept God's commands and demonstrate obedience with their bodies as well as their souls. Because of their obedience, God came to dwell with them at that place.

Trivia Tidbit

Astronomers at the Australian National University tell us that there are around 70 sextillion visible stars in the universe.

As amazing as that is, God offers us an even better option. Jesus Christ offers to purify us and dwell with us through the gift of his Holy Spirit. We also have to obey Christ and be purified to be in his presence. By asking Christ for forgiveness of our sins, we are purified and given the humility necessary to forgive one another. James 5:16 tells us to confess our sins to one another for our mutual good. Just as Moses set boundaries around the mountain to help people obey God, we too must help each other stay pure for God. When we enter into an obedient lifestyle as forgiven people, we find the holiness of God is readily available to us.

Going Deeper Questions

3. When you confess your sins to God and ask for forgiveness, how does it feel to be clean again?

_____

_____

_____

_____

_____

_____

4. If someone asked you why they had to repent of their sins to experience God's holiness, how would you explain it to them?

_____

_____

_____

_____

_____

_____

Day 4

Today's Scripture

Exodus 32; Psalm 99

Key Verse

Extol the LORD our God, and worship at his holy mountain; for the LORD our God is holy.

Psalm 99:9 NRSV

1. What desire caused the people to make the idol while Moses was away?

_____

_____

_____

_____

2. Psalm 99 is a prayer that reveres the Lord for the powerful ways God has blessed Israel. Using this psalm as a model, write a prayer based on your life and God's blessings.

_____

_____

_____

_____

23

Going Deeper

In some ways, the story of the golden calf just seems impossible. How could the Israelites, God's chosen people, create a little idol and assume it had power to protect them at the foot of the mountain where God had come to live with them? The Lord had just brought them out of Egypt in a swirl of miracles and judgments. They came across the desert safely with food and water for everyone, yet they assumed that God had left them because the conversation with Moses was taking too long. Did they think that the Lord would not see them create the idol?

Trivia Tidbit

The earrings that Aaron used to make the golden calf were jewelry that the Egyptians had given the Israelites as God led them out of Egypt (Exodus 12:35-36).

We often think these Israelites fools for forgetting God so quickly after being rescued from generations of slavery, but when we stop and look at our lives, how often do *we* forget God? As Christians, we believe that God dwells with us as the Holy Spirit, yet how often do we do the wrong thing when we think no one is looking? We are set apart for the glory of God, and yet so often we act just like those who do not know the Lord. With the same mouth, we pray to God in the morning, then use God's name as a curse word when stuck in traffic. Our use of time or money does not prioritize God's reign in our lives. While we don't make a lame excuse about a golden calf magically coming out of a fire, our excuses really aren't that much better.

God has offered us help in our battle against sin, yet still we choose to fail. Like the Israelites, we need to realize that our sins are very real and very serious to our Holy God. God gives us the power through the Holy Spirit to fight against our sins, purify ourselves, and prepare for future temptation. Until we remember that the Lord is an ever-present help, we will continue to choose false idols over our majestic God.

Going Deeper Questions

3. We all have sins that tempt us most. What sins cause you to struggle most? What excuses have you told yourself and others to pretend they're not so bad?

_____

_____

_____

_____

_____

_____

4. In what ways can you remind yourself throughout the day that God is present and willing to help you fight your battles with sin?

_____

_____

_____

_____

_____

_____

Today's Scripture

Exodus 40; Isaiah 45

Key Verse

Turn to me and be saved, all you ends of the earth;
for I am God, and there is no other.

Isaiah 45:22 NIV

1. Why do you think God chose to be present in a cloud and in fire during the Exodus?

_____

_____

_____

_____

_____

2. What does Isaiah 45:9 mean to you?

_____

_____

_____

_____

_____

Going Deeper

At the end of Exodus, God literally comes to live with the children of Israel in the tabernacle, their place of worship. The Lord is not in any way limited to this one place but *chooses* to be with the people in the hope that they will love God in return. In a way, this is the point for which all of creation was made, a point where God's people would be in communion with God on earth. God led these people with a cloud by day and fire by night. The people, in turn, followed God's lead and were blessed because of it.

In Isaiah, God promises to "level the mountains" and make it possible for all people to come to the Lord willingly and joyfully. By seeking God, they will find the goodness of life and be saved from harm. This story came to fruition through the death and resurrection of Jesus Christ, when all people, not just the Israelites, gained admission to this dwelling place of God. It is amazing to think that since the fall of Adam and Eve, God had been working to reestablish a relationship of love and fellowship with all people, leading them to the best places and simply dwelling with them.

> ### Trivia Tidbit
>
> *The bread in Exodus 40:22-23 was called the showbread, twelve cakes of bread placed before the Lord representing God's provision for the twelve tribes of Israel. Every week, the bread was replaced, and the old bread was eaten by the priests.*

That plan continues today as God strives to be the center of your life. The Lord has carried this offer of salvation over millennia. Will you let God lead you?

Going Deeper Questions

3. God chooses to be with us. In what ways will you choose to be with God today?

_____

_____

_____

_____

_____

4. In Isaiah, God says that the Lord alone is the one true God. How would you explain this point to those in our world who believe in many gods or no god at all?

_____

_____

_____

_____

_____

God's Fidelity and My Trust

Day 1

Today's Scripture
Deuteronomy 26; Psalm 28

Key Verse
Today you have affirmed that the LORD is your God and that you will walk in His ways, keep His statutes, commands, and ordinances, and obey Him.

Deuteronomy 26:17 HCSB

1. Why does Moses instruct the people of Israel to make this response to God?

_____

_____

_____

_____

_____

2. In what ways do you think of the Lord as your strength and shield?

_____

_____

_____

_____

_____

Going Deeper

In Deuteronomy, Moses gives the Israelites some final instructions about how they should live and worship God. He commands that when the people enter the Promised Land, they are to offer to God ten percent of the food that they grow. This food will go to feed the priests, widows, and orphans of Israel. Imagine what they are thinking. They have been wandering in the desert for forty years, often attacked by other nations as they travel. They are tired and hungry, and now with the Promised Land in sight, God is asking them to give away a tenth of their food. It must be quite a test of their faith.

But God has already promised to provide for them. The Lord has fed them with manna in the desert and kept them safe from warring nations. God has given them everything they needed to survive, and all God has asked for in return is their trust. That is the purpose of their gift. God doesn't need food, money, or time. God desires that we would give it as a sign of our trust in the Lord's faithfulness, to be used to bless others. God promises to be faithful to us when we put our trust in his fidelity.

> **Trivia Tidbit**
>
> *The "wandering Aramean" in Deuteronomy 26:5 refers to the patriarch Jacob, whose two wives were Arameans (see Genesis 28:5; 29:16) and who wandered from Canaan to Haran and back and later moved his family to Egypt.*

Going Deeper Questions

3. When in your life have you had to depend on the Lord for something? How did it turn out, and how did that experience affect you?

_____

_____

_____

_____

_____

4. What can you do to thank God for the blessings that God has provided in your life?

_____

_____

_____

_____

_____

Day 2

Today's Scripture
Luke 4:1-15; Romans 5:1-11

Key Verse

Now hope does not disappoint, because the love of God has been poured out in our hearts by the Holy Spirit who was given to us.

Romans 5:5 NKJV

1. Why do you think Jesus was able to withstand the temptations offered to him?

_____

_____

_____

_____

_____

2. How was Paul able to trust God in the face of suffering?

_____

_____

_____

_____

_____

Going Deeper

Do you ever feel led by God to do something that doesn't make any sense? Maybe you feel called to talk about your faith in Christ with your grumpiest coworker, or perhaps God has asked you to put a lot of time and money into a particular ministry, and you just don't see how it could work out.

Jesus may have felt that way as well when he was led out into the desert for forty days to be tempted by the Devil. Jesus also knew that God would provide for him, because God had already given him a helper. One of the first things that Luke mentions is that Jesus was "filled with the Holy Spirit" before he went out into the wilderness. He could feel the Father's presence through the Holy Spirit, and he knew that through the power of God, all things are possible.

> **Trivia Tidbit**
>
> *Many artists' representations of Satan have portrayed him with horns, a tail, and hooved feet, possibly because Jesus compares sinners to goats in Matthew 25.*

Likewise, Paul tells us in Romans that hope and love are "poured out in our hearts by the Holy Spirit" so that we can persevere in hard times. This same Holy Spirit is promised to all followers of Christ as a Counselor and source of strength in our time of need. The role of the Holy Spirit is to strengthen our mind through Scripture and sustain us when we're in situations that we can't handle alone. The Spirit is always available; we must only open our hearts and continue to ask God to lead us through those tough times.

Going Deeper Questions

3. Recall a time in your life when you were going through a trial or persecution. What did you learn from that experience, and how could it help you depend on God's faithfulness?

_____

_____

_____

_____

_____

_____

4. Is there anyone in your life you would give your life for? What does it mean to you that Jesus died for you, even knowing that you would sin sometimes?

_____

_____

_____

_____

_____

_____

Day 3

Today's Scripture

Luke 5:1-11, 27-39;
2 Corinthians 11:16–12:10

Key Verse

Jesus answered them, "It is not the healthy who need a doctor, but the sick. I have not come to call the righteous, but sinners to repentance."

Luke 5:31-32 NIV

1. How were those called by Jesus to be disciples able to leave everything behind to follow him?

_____

_____

_____

_____

2. Paul suffered greatly to follow his calling. What do you learn about trust from his experiences?

_____

_____

_____

_____

Going Deeper

Some people can create beautiful art or music. Other people can perform impressive athletic feats. Some people are gregarious and friendly, others are intellectual and reverent. There are many attributes that we find worthy of praise, and everyone has a different combination of gifts. One thing we all share in common, however, is a desire to be complimented for the things we do well. That's what makes Paul's "boasting" so unique. He lists all of the things that should make him great among his people, but chooses to focus on the areas where he has been weak or beaten. He says that there is a "thorn in his flesh," possibly a physical problem or a repetitive temptation that he battles again and again. These aren't the things that a person would want to be known for, but Paul says that these weaknesses are essential because they highlight the places where he is most dependent on God. As the children's song says, "They are weak, but He [God] is strong."

> ## Trivia Tidbit
>
> *Tax collectors in the Roman Empire were often native to the area in which they worked and were encouraged to keep a part of the taxes they collected . . . as long as Rome met its tax quota.*

While we love to be praised for our strengths, it is our weaknesses that God fills, giving us something to show others as a real testimony of God's power in our lives. In these areas we know God's faithfulness.

Going Deeper Questions

3. What gifts or area of your life are you most proud of? How can you use these gifts for God's glory?

_____

_____

_____

_____

_____

_____

_____

4. What area of your life do you feel is your greatest weakness? How can you offer that weakness up to God while still striving not to fall into that sin again?

_____

_____

_____

_____

_____

_____

_____

Day 4

Today's Scripture
Luke 7:1-10; Psalm 20

Key Verse

When Jesus heard this, he was amazed at him, and turning to the crowd following him, he said, "I tell you, I have not found such great faith even in Israel!"

Luke 7:9 NIV

1. What enabled the centurion to turn to Jesus for help?

_____

_____

_____

_____

_____

2. Write about a time when the Lord answered you in your distress and how it helped you trust God more in your life.

_____

_____

_____

_____

_____

Going Deeper

You've probably heard or read in the Bible how the Jews sometimes looked down on the Samaritans or the Gentiles for not being God's chosen people. The Pharisees especially had a habit of pointing out the flaws in others, even their fellow Jews. Jesus pointed out that while they were called to be servants of God, they used their power to make themselves appear superior to others. Notice the contrast in this story. A Roman centurion, whose title gave him power and importance, humbles himself before a Jewish rabbi. Jesus is more than willing to bless him because of the humility of his faith. Humility is found in others who met Jesus: the Samaritan woman at the well, the sinful woman who anointed Jesus' feet, and the "unclean" woman who touched Jesus' robe. All of these people found some form of healing from Jesus, yet none of them had anything close to the status of a Pharisee.

> ### Trivia Tidbit
> *While their name may have come from the Latin word for one hundred, centurions at different periods of history commanded anywhere from 30 to 160 troops at a time, according to Adrian Goldsworthy's* Complete Roman Army.

Why is it that God often works in the lives of the least likely people first? Perhaps it is because these people are looking the hardest for a savior. The Pharisees who argued with Jesus had such pride that they felt no need to ask Jesus for anything. Those who felt desperate because of their situation or their sin had nothing but humility and were the most willing to ask for help. These least likely servants give us some of the most touching examples of trust in the Bible. They remind us that trust in God requires humility, and that God is faithful to those who ask.

Going Deeper Questions

3. Is there any area in your life where pride in yourself gets in the way of your trust in God? How can you fight that pride?

_____

_____

_____

_____

_____

_____

4. Is there any person or group in your spiritual life for which you have low respect? Think of one thing that you can learn from this person's faith and write it down. Encourage them in that area at some point.

_____

_____

_____

_____

_____

_____

Today's Scripture

Hebrews 11; Isaiah 45

Key Verse

Now faith is the substance of things hoped for, the evidence of things not seen.

Hebrews 11:1 NKJV

1. Think about the lives of those listed in Hebrews 11. Look up some of their stories in your Bible if your memory needs to be refreshed. What do you learn about God's fidelity from them?

_____

_____

_____

_____

_____

2. What do you think was meant when God said to Isaiah, "Woe to him who strives with his Maker"?

_____

_____

_____

_____

_____

Going Deeper

"By faith" is a phrase that begins nearly every paragraph of Hebrews 11. It is a chant, a motto, that walks through the stories of the Old Testament. It serves to point out the driving force behind all of Israel's heroes: they lived "by faith." God had promised them all, through Abraham, that a Savior was coming to bring peace and prosperity to the world. They lived and served God faithfully, trusting "by faith" that the Lord would deliver on this promise. They passed on that faith to their descendants, from parent to child through the ages, waiting in faith for the coming Messiah of Abraham's seed.

> ### Trivia Tidbit
>
> *Enoch and Elijah are the only two people in the Bible to be bodily assumed into heaven without dying.*
>
> *Incidentally, President Calvin Coolidge had a pet goose named Enoch, according to Mo Rocca's book* All the Presidents' Pets.

But how did they come to this faith? How did they maintain it through the generations of oppression and brokenness, when their kingdoms fell and their people were enslaved? The only thing that sustained them was their trust in a God who had manifested love and faithfulness first. This passage in Hebrews is a list not just of human faith but of God's faithfulness. It was God who blessed their lives. It was God who sustained them in hard times. It was God who freed them from Egypt and fed them in the desert. Finally, it was God who faithfully provided the promise of a Messiah and gave us God's Son, Jesus Christ, who is faithful and just to forgive us our sins. Like the great saints of the Old Testament, we too can remember God's past faithfulness in our lives and trust God as we wait for the coming of our Lord . . . "by faith."

Going Deeper Questions

3. How did the faithful in Hebrews live in anticipation of the Messiah? How can we look forward to Christ's return with the same passion that the faithful had in waiting for the Messiah?

_____

_____

_____

_____

_____

_____

4. How can you best celebrate Christ's life and resurrection as you await his Second Coming?

_____

_____

_____

_____

_____

_____

_____

Week Three

God's Purity and My Humility

Day
1

Key Verse

Therefore he is able to save completely those who come to God through him, because he always lives to intercede for them.
                                                    Hebrews 7:25 NIV

1. What do you learn about God's purity from Isaiah's vision?

_____

_____

_____

_____

_____

2. Why does Isaiah react with fear to an encounter with God?

_____

_____

_____

_____

_____

Going Deeper

This passage in Isaiah is the only one in the Bible that mentions "seraphim" or "seraphs" by name. All we know about them is that they have six wings. Perhaps the appearance of these heavenly beings is similar to human form since one of them had hands to carry the hot coal to Isaiah's lips. However, there are still things that we can learn from them. The seraphim spend all of their time serving in the presence of God. Yet, despite an eternity in the Lord's service, they are still awed by the power and majesty of the Creator God. With their wings, they cover their face and feet, too reverent even to look upon the face of God. They hover in the air, too modest even to walk on the same ground as the I AM. They are humbled because they have seen and know that the Lord our God is mighty and holy. Isaiah realizes this holiness immediately. He feels like the beauty and purity of God is pressing him to the ground. If the angels are not holy enough to stand in the Lord's presence, how can a sinful man like him hope to survive?

> ### Trivia Tidbit
>
> *The name* Levi *comes from the Hebrew word for "joined." Hebrews tells us* Melchizedek *means "King of Righteousness," which could also be rendered "King of Justice."*

The good news is that God does allow us into the divine presence, not because we deserve it but because Christ has already atoned for our sins. Sometimes we can become so used to this privilege that we take it for granted. Christian T-shirts declare "Jesus is our homeboy," but we forget that YAHWEH is our pure and holy God, before whom even angels bow. If even the seraphim cover themselves before the Lord's holiness, should we not humble ourselves as well?

Going Deeper Questions

3. In what ways was Melchizedek a foreshadowing of Christ and his ministry?

_____

_____

_____

_____

_____

_____

_____

4. Recall a time in your past where something happened that helped you grow in your relationship with God. In what ways did God guide you and make it possible for that situation to occur?

_____

_____

_____

_____

_____

_____

_____

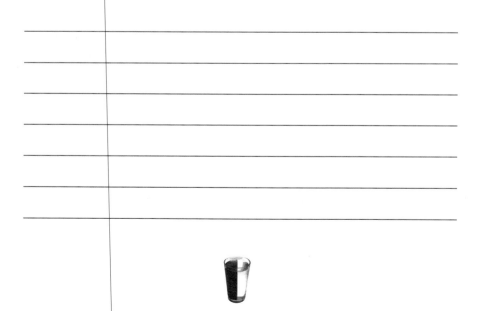

Day 2

Today's Scripture
Hebrews 8; Psalm 51

Key Verse

My sacrifice, O God, is a broken spirit; a broken and contrite heart you, God, will not despise.

Psalm 51:17 TNIV

1. What is the function of a priest in the Old Testament?

_____

_____

_____

_____

_____

2. What does the author of Hebrews find distinctive about Jesus?

_____

_____

_____

_____

_____

Going Deeper

The Greek philosopher Plato described reality and representations in his Allegory of the Cave. In this story, people living in a cave see shadows of things on the wall—the shadow of a bird, for example. Because they have never seen a bird, they assume that the shadow must be a real bird. Then one day, someone gets to leave the cave, and he sees an actual bird for the first time. He learns that the shadows in the cave are simply a representation of something. The shadow is an outline of a bird, but not the real thing.

A similar idea is found in this chapter of Hebrews. The priests of the Old Testament were a representation of God's holiness and purity. They helped connect the Israelites to God. They made sacrifices for the people to cover their sins and to give praise to God. They made an earthly representation of the worship of God that takes place in heaven.

Trivia Tidbit

Plato's Allegory of the Cave was a part of his most famous work, The Republic, *written around 380 B.C. In comparison, Hebrews was probably written around A.D. 64.*

Then Jesus came as the full reality of that worship. Where the priests connected people to an unseen God, Jesus was God in the flesh. While the priests had to offer sacrifices every day for the people's sins, Jesus offered himself as the once-and-for-all sacrifice for the sins of the world. The priests served in the holy place of the Temple. Jesus *was* the Holy of Holies. The priests did the heavenly work of representing God to the people. Christ brought the purity of God to us in a way that was tangible.

Going Deeper Questions

3. Recall a time when you have asked God for something and he has answered your prayer in a way you wouldn't have expected. Write it down.

_____

_____

_____

_____

_____

_____

4. How have you seen God's promises fulfilled in your life? Are there any promises that you have made to God or others that you have yet to fulfill?

_____

_____

_____

_____

_____

_____

_____

Today's Scripture

Hebrews 9; Luke 7:36-50

Key Verse

Therefore, I tell you, her many sins have been forgiven—as her great love has shown. But whoever has been forgiven little loves little.

Luke 7:47 NIV

1. Why is Jesus' death on the cross a distinctive sacrifice?

2. If you were in the room in Luke 7, would you feel more like the woman at Jesus' feet or Simon the Pharisee? Why?

Going Deeper

This passage in Luke may be one of the most compelling stories in all of Scripture for its portrayal of our fallen nature in the face of God's purity and of Christ's love for all sinners. First, we see Jesus eating dinner at a Pharisee's house. They feel superior to Jesus. In the Gospels these men spend most of their time trying to trick Jesus and plot his downfall, yet he dines with them just as he does with the tax collectors. Jesus welcomes them to the table where he is eating. He shares a meal with them. In Jesus' culture, this was an offer of community and friendship.

In contrast to the Pharisees is the woman who washes Jesus' feet. While this may seem a small act, it was incredible for the time period. The most common means of transportation in that day was walking in sandaled feet along filthy roads. Pack animals and livestock going to market traveled the same roads, and sanitation was surely not of the highest quality. It is easy to understand why the job of foot washing was reserved for the lowest servant of a household. Yet this woman recognized her sinfulness compared to the Lord's purity, and willfully took the job upon herself. Not only did she wash his feet, she anointed them with oil. In that culture, an anointing by oil was an act of honor. It was done at the crowning of a new king and as a way of preparing a body for burial. In Jesus, she recognized something greater than herself, greater than anyone she had ever met. She did not know his full identity or how he would die, yet her instincts were on target. By humbly anointing him with oil, she proclaimed Jesus both a king and a Savior.

> **Trivia Tidbit**
>
> *The Roman Empire had the best-engineered sewer systems in the ancient world, with scholars estimating that the earliest sewers were built in Rome more than 700 years before Christ.*

Going Deeper Questions

3. Who do you relate to most in this passage: Simon, who learns Christ's love through explanation, or the woman, who understands by experience?

_____

_____

_____

_____

_____

4. Doing Christ's will in our lives helps both to humble us before God and to build up his body, the church. Where in your life could you humble yourself and better serve Christ and his church?

_____

_____

_____

_____

_____

Day 4

Today's Scripture
Hebrews 10; Isaiah 53

Key Verse

For by one sacrifice he has made perfect forever those who are being made holy.

Hebrews 10:14 NIV

1. Why does the author of Hebrews say Christ's followers should have confidence in their salvation?

_____

_____

_____

_____

_____

2. What does Isaiah's prophecy of the suffering servant teach us about Christ and the purity of God's holiness?

_____

_____

_____

_____

_____

Going Deeper

References to sheep can be found throughout the Bible, from Genesis through Revelation. Shepherding was an important occupation in the ancient world because sheep provided both warm wool for clothing and nutritious meat for food. Sheep were also integral to the Jewish religious life as one of the key sacrifices to God. While bulls were also sacrificed to the Lord, they were far more expensive. Sheep, on the other hand, were available to people of almost any economic status. Once a year, the high priest of Israel would sacrifice an "unblemished" sheep for the atonement of all of Israel's sins that year. The blood of this sheep would then be sprinkled on the Ark of the Covenant, and the sacrificial lamb would be eaten by the priests.

> **Trivia Tidbit**
>
> *When the author of Hebrews says in 10:22 that the people's hearts are "sprinkled clean," he is alluding to Exodus 29, where the priests' clothes were purified with a sprinkling of the blood from the sacrificial ram. On the Day of Atonement, the Ark of the Covenant was also sprinkled with blood.*

All of these traditions would have been prominent in the minds of Isaiah and those he prophesied to in this passage. We call Jesus the "Lamb of God" because he was without sin. He alone was perfect and unblemished, a pure enough sacrifice to be offered in place of the sins of the world. Just like the spotless lamb on the Day of Atonement, Christ was offered for the sins of the people. When Christians participate in the sacrament of Communion, we are offered a chance to be forgiven and purified as we remember Christ's purity, his sacrifice for our sake, and his love for all humanity. This opportunity comes to us not once a year, but as often as we attend to the Lord's Supper.

Going Deeper Questions

3. The God of Creation humbled himself to the point of death on the cross for each of us. What response can you make in your life to thank him for such love?

_____

_____

_____

_____

_____

_____

4. Communion is our chance to praise Christ for being our perfect and spotless lamb. In what ways do you experience Holy Communion as a time to remember and celebrate Jesus' sacrifice? How does this impact your life?

_____

_____

_____

_____

_____

_____

Day 5

Today's Scripture
Hebrews 12; Luke 18:9-14

Key Verse

Let us throw off everything that hinders and the sin that so easily entangles. And let us run with perseverance the race marked out for us.

Hebrews 12:1b NIV

1. What does the author of Hebrews call us to do?

_____

_____

_____

_____

_____

2. Write about a time in your life when you acted like the Pharisee or the tax collector in the parable. What resulted from that time?

_____

_____

_____

_____

_____

Going Deeper

The Pharisee in Jesus' parable seems incredibly pompous in the way he talks about himself. To us, he comes off as annoying, self-absorbed, and a braggart, but to the people of Jesus' time, he was the epitome of a religious man. While Israelites were required to fast once every year on the Day of Atonement, Pharisees fasted twice a week to show that they were truly pious. A Pharisee would sometimes put ashes on his head to let everyone know that he was fasting that day. Similarly, the Pharisees were exacting in how much they gave, measuring out even one tenth of their spices to donate to the Lord. Yet they often gave for worldly recognition rather than from godly humility.

> ## Trivia Tidbit
>
> *One forerunner of the Pharisees, Judas Maccabeus, was a staunch opponent of athletic competitions because most sports were imported from the Greek culture.*

Jesus even proclaimed that a poor woman who gave less than a penny gave more than all the Pharisees combined because she gave all she had, and without any fanfare.

Finally, when he prayed, this Pharisee stood up and loudly proclaimed his "goodness" so that all could hear. In Matthew 6:5-8, Jesus specifically denounces this kind of prayer, calling those who practice it "hypocrites" and "pagans." God understands our motives. Christ was most aware of those who came to him with an understanding of their own brokenness and who no longer wanted anything but healing from their illness or sinfulness. When we come to Christ with such humility, we bring an availability that enables God to heal us and make us pure.

Going Deeper Questions

3. Examine your motives. In what ways do you need to change your motives about prayer, church, and serving God?

_____

_____

_____

_____

_____

_____

_____

4. What aspect of God's character do you find most humbling and most worthy of praise? Write out a prayer thanking God for that aspect.

_____

_____

_____

_____

_____

_____

God's Authority and My Obedience

Today's Scripture

Joshua 24:1-22; Romans 10

Key Verse

For it is with your heart that you believe and are justified, and it is with your mouth that you profess your faith and are saved.

Romans 10:10 NIV

1. Why does Joshua make such a forceful challenge and covenant with the people of Israel before his death?

_____

_____

_____

_____

_____

2. What does it mean to "submit to God's righteousness" in Romans 10:3? What would this mean in your life?

_____

_____

_____

_____

_____

Going Deeper

Paul begins this chapter of Romans showing how great a love and respect he has for the people of Israel. As a Jew, he understands Israel's place as the chosen nation of the Lord, and his heart yearns for their full understanding of salvation. In essence, Paul commends their spirit in following the law but wishes to redirect their zeal toward the true Messiah, Jesus Christ. The Jews already understood the need for obedience to God. For centuries, they had followed the Law of Moses with precision. In addition, when the Law wasn't clear enough, they constructed rigid laws of their own to fulfill both the spirit and the letter of the Mosaic Law.

Paul recognized in his fellow Jews the strength of their obedience and boldly tried to refocus their efforts from following the Law to following Christ. In the same way, we sometimes need to refocus our efforts of obedience. Obedience that pleases God happens when we are in concert with God's will. Our focus is not on keeping the rules of God but on living in a relationship with God. It means that we are living in such a vital relationship with Christ that it does not occur to us to be anything other than obedient. What brings him joy brings us joy. What he finds offensive, we find offensive. And our obedience is not done to prove anything to God or to procure us a place in heaven. We understand that our salvation is already secure in the righteousness of Christ alone. Our faith in him is transforming our character and our actions in such a way that we are simply reflecting the joy of our salvation.

Trivia Tidbit

By tracing back the heritage of Abraham's father, Terah, we learn that Abraham was the great-great-great-great-great-great-great-great-grandson of Noah.

Going Deeper Questions

3. What rules or expectations in Christianity are you most confused by? Write down what you think these rules mean and discuss them with your small group or other church members.

_____

_____

_____

_____

_____

_____

4. In what areas of your life do you still struggle to do the will of God? What would help you as you face this struggle?

_____

_____

_____

_____

_____

_____

_____

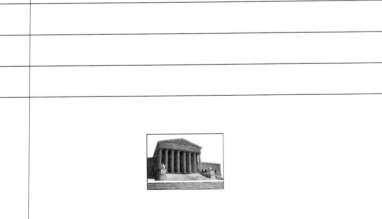

Day 2

Today's Scripture
Luke 9:28-36; Romans 12

Key Verse

Do not conform to the pattern of this world, but be transformed by the renewing of your mind. Then you will be able to test and approve what God's will is—his good, pleasing and perfect will.

Romans 12:2 TNIV

1. Write down what Peter might have told the other disciples after returning from the mountain with Jesus and what conclusions they may have drawn from this experience.

_____

_____

_____

_____

2. What are some of Paul's directions about the Christian life, and how do they apply to you?

_____

_____

_____

_____

Going Deeper

Imagine you were Peter, James, and John in this story, waking up from a nap to find their master, Jesus, chatting with Moses and Elijah! As incredible as that would be for us nowadays, it would be even more surreal for the Jewish disciples. For them, Moses is a national hero and then some, the man who led Israel out of bondage in Egypt and received the Law of the Israelites directly from God. In addition, it was prophesied in Malachi that Elijah would return to herald the coming of the Day of the Lord. This is an unimaginable honor for the disciples to witness, and they hardly know what to say. In an attempt to capture the grandness of it all, Peter offers to set up a tabernacle for each of the men, esteeming Moses and Elijah on the same level with Jesus. Even before he finishes speaking, God finds a way to stop Peter and the others. God encloses the whole assembly in a cloud and claims Jesus alone as "my Son." God gives a commandment: "listen to him." Jesus is the one God has chosen, and is worthy of worship.

> ### Trivia Tidbit
>
> *Mountaintops play heavily into Christian history. Moses and Elijah talked to God on Mt. Sinai, Moses died on Mt. Nebo, and Abraham almost sacrificed his son Isaac on Mt. Moriah.*

Perhaps sometimes we do the same thing as Peter. We see the blessings that God has given us, and we place them all on an equal pedestal in our minds. We may thank God for our spouse, our family, and our job, but we show the same level of love and appreciation to the gifts as we do to the Giver. What God shows us in this passage is that we need to stop, focus on Christ, and listen to him. We can set aside our activities to make sure that we are partaking of moments when Jesus is worshiped and his wisdom for our lives is considered carefully. Enjoying such holy moments is an act of faith and love.

Going Deeper Questions

3. If the disciples did not tell anyone about Christ's transfiguration until much later, what was the purpose of this miracle? Why was it necessary?

_____

_____

_____

_____

_____

4. In what ways do you need to be transformed to be more obedient to God? How can you effect those changes this week?

_____

_____

_____

_____

_____

_____

Day 3

Key Verse

Owe no one anything except to love one another, for he who loves another has fulfilled the law.

Romans 13:8 NKJV

1. What meaning did the disciples take from this miracle?

_____

_____

_____

_____

_____

2. Why is obedience to God so important to Paul?

_____

_____

_____

_____

_____

Going Deeper

Looking at Romans 13, we might assume that Paul is a little naive about government and the ethical conflicts Christians can sometimes face living in the broader society. But surely Paul understood it well, having lived under Emperors Claudius and Caligula and three years of Nero at this point. The purpose of this passage is to impress upon Christians not the idea that rulers are infallible but the truth that God can be trusted. Human leaders will always fail in one way or another. We have free will, and at times, every one of us uses this will in a way that God did not intend.

When the leaders of countries go astray, it can affect many people adversely. Yet God is the ultimate authority in all things, not just in the lives of Christians. While leaders may fall, God promises to carry God's children through the rough times and eventually grant them a place in heaven. In the Old Testament there are examples of the Lord using rulers who believed they were gods to accomplish Yahweh's ends. God redeems history in a variety of ways, even using the Jewish Exile in the Babylonian era to ensure the future of Judaism as it spread throughout the known world of the time.

> **Trivia Tidbit**
>
> *Dr. Donald B. DeYoung states that the Sea of Galilee lies in the Great Rift Valley, which acts as a wind tunnel for passing air currents, causing storms in that region to be sudden and incredibly powerful.*

Certainly, God could have changed all the bad things in history, but to do so would have done away with the free will of the people at that time. Our free will is balanced by God's redemptive capacity, turning even the impact of evil into something that can later work for good in the lives of those who love the Lord. God allows us to have rulers in our lives and to make our own decisions, but God's greatest desire is that we open ourselves to the rule of Christ in our lives. Living under his Lordship changes our priorities, our loyalties, and our future.

Going Deeper Questions

3. In your life, how have you seen God bring about blessings and hope in the midst of turmoil?

_____

_____

_____

_____

_____

_____

4. In what areas of your life do you feel called to give God more control or authority?

_____

_____

_____

_____

_____

_____

_____

Today's Scripture

Luke 9:1-9; Luke 10:1-24;
1 Thessalonians 4:1-12

Key Verses

*For God did not call us to be impure, but to live a holy life.
Therefore, anyone who rejects this instruction does not reject
a human being but God, the very God who gives you his
Holy Spirit.*

1 Thessalonians 4:7-8 NIV

1. What authority did Jesus give his disciples?

_____

_____

_____

_____

_____

2. Why would obedience to Jesus be so essential to their ministry?

_____

_____

_____

_____

_____

Going Deeper

Can you imagine suddenly leaving your home, your job, and your family to go somewhere you may have never been and preach to people who may not want to hear? That sounds hard enough, but Jesus asks for even more trust in these passages from Luke. He asks that his disciples take nothing with them—no money, no extra clothes, not even shoes! Why would Jesus ask them not to take supplies that they already had, even the most basic of life's necessities? Because following God's plan still takes trust—LOTS of trust.

While you may not be called to a life of nomadic evangelism, Christ asks a lot from Christians by modern standards. He desires that we freely offer our tithe and offering, a portion of our hard-earned money, back to him. He expects us to abstain from actions, words, and thoughts that our culture claims are perfectly natural, even essential to express, such as anger, vulgarity, or contempt for persons or groups. He commands that we care for the less fortunate by serving with our time and talent. Even harder, Christ calls us all to love our enemies.

> ### Trivia Tidbit
>
> *According to the International Standard Bible Encyclopedia, Bethsaida was a small fishing village near Capernaum on the Sea of Galilee. Its name means "house of fishing" in Hebrew, and it was the home of the disciples Peter, Andrew, and Philip.*

Yet in all this, the Lord provides for us in our time of need, just as he did for the first disciples. Dependent on Christ, we learn that through him we can learn to enjoy serving others, loving others, and following his calling. The format of God's calling may have changed over time, but the message remains the same. We are called to offer everything to Christ's authority, and in turn he will provide for us and use us to bless the world.

Going Deeper Questions

3. What in your life—physical or spiritual—is the hardest thing for you to give up to the Lord? How can you work toward offering that to God?

_____

_____

_____

_____

_____

_____

4. Recall a time in your life when you surrendered something to God. How did that situation work out, and what did it teach you about God's sovereignty?

_____

_____

_____

_____

_____

Today's Scripture

Exodus 20:1-21; Psalm 50

Key Verse

And the heavens proclaim his righteousness, for he is a God of justice.

Psalm 50:6 TNIV

1. List the Ten Commandments. Which one seems the easiest to keep? Which one seems the hardest?

_____

_____

_____

_____

_____

_____

2. What is the relationship with God described in Psalm 50:14-15?

_____

_____

_____

_____

_____

Going Deeper

Slow down. Stay left. Don't touch that.

Most people don't like rules; they get in the way of what we want to be doing. The problem is that all rules are put in place for a reason, usually for people's protection. God's rules are exactly that: a means of protecting us from our sinful nature.

When God gave Moses the Ten Commandments, he had just led the people out of slavery in Egypt and was taking them to a land where they would be surrounded by other cultures that followed other gods and other sets of rules. God provided a set of rules that would keep the Israelites pure and set apart from the nations of Canaan, who had deplorable practices. Not only did the Law protect the Israelites from local customs like child sacrifice and temple prostitution, it also gave them a way to worship God. It was a sacrifice not of dove or lamb but of the heart that every Israelite could make every day.

> **Trivia Tidbit**
>
> *In the Old Testament, God appeared to the Israelites in a number of different ways, including a burning bush, a tall cloud, a pillar of fire, and a thunder and lightning storm.*

Just as God brought the chosen people out of Egypt long ago, God has the power today to bring us out of our sinful ways and into the beauty of the divine presence. This is the value of God's laws. They protect us from the evils of this world and set us apart as servants of the Lord. Thus our obedience is a shield against worldliness and a pathway to the worship of our God.

Going Deeper Questions

3. Are there any "rules" in Christianity that you struggle with? Write down how these laws may help you worship God or protect you from worldly influence.

_____

_____

_____

_____

_____

_____

4. Choose one of the Ten Commandments. In what ways can you better live out this commandment in your daily life?

_____

_____

_____

_____

_____

_____

God's Righteousness and My Work for Justice

Today's Scripture
Luke 19:28-48; Psalm 96

Key Verse
"Blessed is the King who comes in the name of the Lord!"
Peace in heaven and glory in the highest!

Luke 19:38 NKJV

1. Find the meaning of "righteousness" in the dictionary. Write it in your journal.

_____

_____

_____

_____

_____

2. Why did Jesus become so angry with the sellers in the Temple?

_____

_____

_____

_____

_____

Going Deeper

This passage in Luke describes the beginning of the last week of Jesus' life before his crucifixion. Jesus knew that during the upcoming Passover festival, he would be betrayed and die for the salvation of all people. Everything he did beforehand, he did with purpose.

As Jesus approached Jerusalem, he stopped at the Mount of Olives and sent two disciples ahead for a donkey that had never before had a rider. He would return to this place, to a garden called Gethsemane, to pray before his arrest. As he approached Jerusalem on the heights above the city, Jesus paused to take in the scene. He could see the homes, shops, and people below him. Jesus wept for the city and its inhabitants as a father weeps for his children. He wept not because of his impending death, but because the people of Jerusalem had been waiting for generations for a Messiah and now would not accept the one God had sent. Jesus also knew something else that he shared with his disciples: it would be a few short decades before the capital of Judah was destroyed without realizing its King had come.

Jesus went to the Temple, the holiest of places in Israel's history. The presence of God was said to have dwelt there. In the outermost area, where the Gentiles were to have a place for prayer and worship, merchants had set up shop, selling animals to be sacrificed or exchanging Roman coins into currency seen as cleaner or holier. Jesus chased away those who would turn the Temple into a place of profit that often took advantage of pilgrims from far away.

> **Trivia Tidbit**
>
> *The destruction that Jesus prophesied is probably the one that Jewish historian Josephus recorded in A.D. 70, when the city and the temple were torn down brick by brick by the Romans, leaving only the Western Wall of the Temple standing.*

Jesus' desire was to return the Temple to its rightful place as a house of prayer, and in doing so he reclaimed space for the Gentiles and made it a more holy and just place for all who came to worship.

Going Deeper Questions

3. Was Jesus justified in throwing out those who were selling in the Temple? How would you defend him if you were his lawyer?

_____

_____

_____

_____

_____

4. Has someone you love ever been hurt by his or her decisions, either physically or emotionally? How did you deal with the situation? Describe what you imagine it must be like for God to see one of us heading down a bad path.

_____

_____

_____

_____

_____

Day 2

Today's Scripture
Luke 11:37-54; Micah 6

Key Verse

He has shown you, O mortal, what is good. And what does the LORD require of you? To act justly and to love mercy and to walk humbly with your God.

Micah 6:8 NIV

1. List the objections Jesus had to the Pharisees and teachers of the Law. Why was he willing to put himself at risk to say these things?

_____

_____

_____

_____

_____

2. What does Micah say the Lord requires of the faithful?

_____

_____

_____

_____

_____

Going Deeper

Wow! Both Jesus and Micah use some pretty harsh imagery for what seems like a small offense. In Jesus' case, the request of the Pharisee to wash his hands before dinner elicited a strong response. But there's far more to this story than hygiene. The Pharisee here was talking about a ritual washing called *mayim rishonim*, which the Pharisees claimed symbolized chastity and purity. In fact, not doing so could supposedly cause divine retribution of poverty or death. There is no command for this found in Scripture; the Pharisees taught this as a part of their tradition. They felt it was equivalent to a sacred decree given to the people by God.

The scribes and elders interpreted new rules and required them of the people, yet the scribes themselves didn't follow the bigger precepts of the Law, such as justice to the poor or love of others. They were happy to be seen at the front of the synagogues with all the perks that came with their station in Jewish society. Jesus calls them equal to their forefathers in destroying the prophets. While their ancestors killed the prophets, the Pharisees of Jesus' time were ignoring their God-given message.

> ## Trivia Tidbit
>
> *First Kings 16:30 claims that the Israelite king Ahab (mentioned in Micah 6:16) "did more evil in the eyes of the LORD" than all of the kings before him. At his death, dogs licked up his blood, which was a sign of his shame and sinfulness.*

Micah's words remind us that the most important sacrifice we can offer God is our hearts. And that's the point for us. We don't make the rules; we are the followers. We are to be focused on the things that God desires that are stated plainly in Scripture: love and justice for all people, so that everyone will know the blessings of righteousness and the love of God for their lives.

Going Deeper Questions

3. What kind of people do you sometimes feel "don't fit" at church? Have you ever been one of them? How can you reach out to those people who are different from you?

_____

_____

_____

_____

_____

4. What big precepts of faith (justice, love, and so forth) do you think the church should be showing more of? How will you as a church member help that happen?

_____

_____

_____

_____

_____

_____

Day 3

Today's Scripture
Luke 12:13-21; Isaiah 42:1-9

Key Verse

I, Yahweh, have called You for a righteous purpose, and I will hold You by Your hand. I will keep You and appoint You to be a covenant for the people and a light to the nations.

Isaiah 42:6 HCSB

1. Why doesn't Jesus care about the man's request in Luke 12:13?

_____

_____

_____

_____

_____

2. What does Isaiah prophesy about the Messiah?

_____

_____

_____

_____

_____

Going Deeper

The rich man in Jesus' parable sounds pretty smart, doesn't he? He's storing up for the future, planning ahead, and he seems to have it all together. He understands that sometimes bad things happen and it's good to be prepared. The problem comes out right at the end when he says he is doing it just to "eat, drink and enjoy [him]self." Suddenly it becomes clear that he's not saving up to serve God and thank the Lord for his blessings. This man is living to get as much "stuff" as he can in life.

> ## Trivia Tidbit
>
> *Rabbis were the educated individuals of Jesus' time, trained in the Jewish Law. Thus they were sometimes called upon as legal counselors in civil matters such as inheritances, as in Luke 12:13.*

The idea of "eat, drink, and be merry" was a reflection of the Epicureans, pagan Greek philosophers who believed that God had created the world, then left men and women to their own designs. Epicureans believed that the point of life was to enjoy all the pleasures that they could in life because there was no afterlife for them. They had no boundaries and desired to indulge themselves in any way practical. This kind of thinking runs counter to the teaching of Christ. Christians believe in a loving, personal God who cares for everyone and wants everyone's needs to be met, both here and in eternity. We are invited to join God in the pleasure of serving and loving others as a pathway to joy.

Going Deeper Questions

With his focus on his present life and material wealth, the man in this parable had not cared for those around him or answered God's call to bless others. Jesus points out that in the blink of an eye, this world as we know it could be gone, and only our service to God will remain.

3. The world says that our security for the future is found in money, power, job security, or any number of other things. What material thing is the most difficult for you to give up to God?

_____

_____

_____

_____

_____

4. We've all been blessed with certain amounts of money, time, and talents. How often do you use these for the things God is calling you to? In what ways might you do more to help God and others?

_____

_____

_____

_____

_____

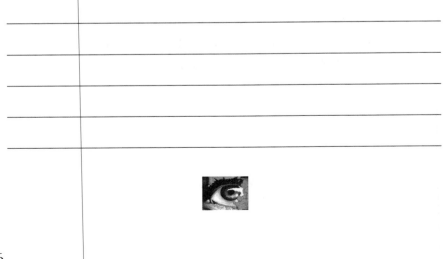

Day 4

Today's Scripture
Luke 14:1-24; Isaiah 51:1-8

Key Verse

Listen to me, you who pursue righteousness and who seek the LORD: Look to the rock from which you were cut and to the quarry from which you were hewn.

Isaiah 51:1 NIV

1. Why did Jesus heal the man when he knew the Sabbath regulations prohibited work?

2. What is the connection between God's righteousness and our work for justice?

Going Deeper

"That's not the way I raised you." Maybe you heard that phrase once or twice when you were a kid. Whether you were putting your elbows on the table when you ate or putting a frog in your sister's pillowcase, there was most likely some point in your history when you did something your parents thought you shouldn't do.

Now that you're grown up, you can probably look back and see all the ways that you *are* like your parents. A lot of these similarities are good. That's because parents are incredibly important to how our attitudes and actions are shaped as children. Isaiah told the people of Israel to look to their spiritual ancestors, such as Abraham and Sarah, and imitate their faithfulness. Abraham was made righteous by God according to his faith and trust in God, which enabled him to follow God's will at all times.

We too should look to our Christian family, both biological and spiritual, for advice about how to be better Christians.

> **Trivia Tidbit**
>
> *The Pharisees had strict rules about what was considered "work" on a Sabbath. For instance, according to the* People's New Testament *commentary, they believed that on the day of rest, people should not be allowed to set a broken arm.*

No matter how long we've been around, or how much we think we have figured out, there is much to learn about being a follower of Christ. We need one another to spur us along to godliness. So pray for other Christians, encourage them, and give God the praise for all the "godparents" provided in your life.

Going Deeper Questions

3. Why is each of the excuses given in Jesus' Parable of the Banquet a poor argument for missing the feast?

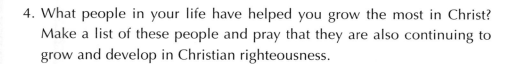

4. What people in your life have helped you grow the most in Christ? Make a list of these people and pray that they are also continuing to grow and develop in Christian righteousness.

Day 5

Key Verse

*And those who know your name put their trust in you, for you, O L*ORD*, have not forsaken those who seek you.*

Psalm 9:10 NRSV

1. Why didn't the rich man attend to Lazarus when he had the opportunity?

_____

_____

_____

2. Recount a time when you embraced the opportunity to serve someone in need. What did you gain or lose from this experience?

_____

_____

_____

3. Write out the part of Psalm 9 that teaches you the most about God's righteousness or our work for justice.

_____

_____

_____

Going Deeper

In the Book of Psalms, one of the repeated refrains is that God is a mighty judge and a protector of the oppressed. The writers of the psalms often cry out to God, pointing out that people who do wrong seem to be prosperous while people who follow God are taken advantage of by those who ignore justice or who have more power. These prayers cry out for the God of justice to put an end to the tyranny of the wicked.

Contrast this to other refrains found in the psalms that are jubilant praises of those who have seen God's justice done. These celebrate moments when "enemies retreat" and the "wicked are destroyed." So often we want to take the role of the judge rather than do the work of justice in the world.

Jesus told a parable of a rich man who never attended to Lazarus, a poor man who lived near the gate of his home. One can picture the rich man judging Lazarus, stating why he is in such poverty and what should be done about it. Yet the rich man is never motivated to do a charitable and just act such as offering Lazarus a cup of water or a portion of food. Jesus taught his disciples to leave judgment of others to God and to join him in works of mercy and justice to those who lack resources or opportunity.

> **Trivia Tidbit**
>
> *The rich man in Jesus' parable is never given a name, but the poor man is aptly named Lazarus, from the Hebrew name* Eleazar, *which means "God is my help."*

Going Deeper Questions

4. What is the difference between making a judgment regarding others and judging others? How are we to do the work of justice in the world without judging others?

_____

_____

_____

_____

_____

_____

_____

5. What are some things that you live with each day, things that might be like Lazarus by your gate? What do you sense God is calling you to do as a result?

_____

_____

_____

_____

_____

_____

_____

God's Graciousness and My Love of Others

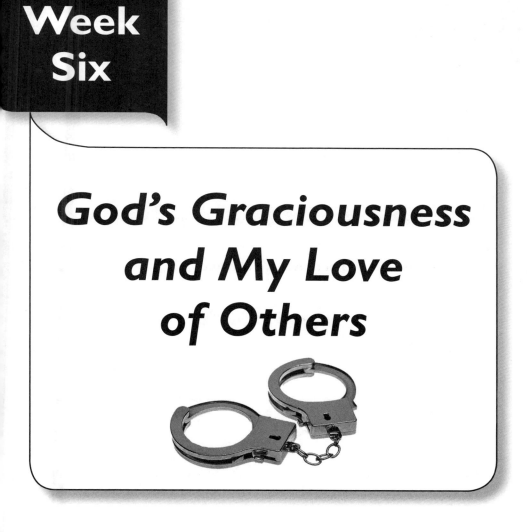

Today's Scripture

1 John 1; Psalm 103

Key Verse

But if we walk in the light, as he is in the light, we have fellowship with one another, and the blood of Jesus, his Son, purifies us from all sin.

1 John 1:7 NIV

1. What, according to the author of 1 John, is the relationship between God's grace to us and our love of each other?

_____

_____

_____

_____

_____

2. The psalmist shares some of the benefits of knowing God. List some of the ways God's grace is present in your life.

_____

_____

_____

_____

_____

Going Deeper

Have you ever found yourself stumbling around in a dark room, trying to find something? Maybe it's the middle to the night and you have to go to the bathroom. Maybe you're trying to find a missing sock on your way out the door. Or maybe you're just looking for the light switch. Whatever the case, the darkness makes it much harder to get anything done, and if you stub your toe on the furniture, it can be a lot more painful too.

Now imagine that someone has watching you fumble around in the dark and offers to turn on the light for you. Wouldn't that make things a lot easier? Jesus has offered to be the light for all of us. 1 John 1:4-5 says that the life given by Jesus Christ is "the light of all mankind. The light shines in the darkness, and the darkness has not overcome it."

Today's passage tells us that we can't be a light for ourselves. The more we pretend that we can see in the dark, the more we hurt ourselves. In daily life, that means banged shins and angry words. In our spiritual lives, when we try to do things on our own power, the Bible says, "the truth is not in us." When we stop stumbling around, we can ask God to take control and accept the love of God for our lives. It is like a light bulb illuminating our lives. God wants to guide us through the dark, but we have to accept what God is offering, just like we turn on a light when we wake up each day. When that is present in our lives, it is a light we can share with others.

> **Trivia Tidbit**
>
> The psalmist's term "the Pit" refers to Sheol, the Hebrew "realm of the dead." This afterlife destination where both the righteous and unrighteous dead seem to await the Lord's judgment is mentioned in both Job and Jonah in addition to the Psalms.

Going Deeper Questions

3. In what areas of your life do you often fumble in the dark rather than let others see what's hidden there? In what ways can you let Jesus bring light to those areas?

_____

_____

_____

_____

_____

_____

_____

4. Who in your life can you help by shining the light of God's love? How will you go about sharing that light?

_____

_____

_____

_____

_____

_____

_____

Day 2

Today's Scripture
Luke 8:26-39; Psalm 98

Key Verse

"Return home and tell how much God has done for you." So the man went away and told all over town how much Jesus had done for him.

Luke 8:39 TNIV

1. Why did the man healed by Jesus want to join him? How could telling others what God had done for him be an act of love for others?

_____

_____

_____

_____

_____

2. After reading Psalm 98, write a prayer of thanksgiving for God's grace using examples from your own life.

_____

_____

_____

_____

_____

Going Deeper

One of the many things to notice about the story of the demon-possessed man is how everyone reacts to his healing. The people of the town have tried for years to contain this man, apparently resorting to chains and guards to keep themselves safe. Yet when he is finally freed of his affliction, the people are even more scared. Perhaps they are afraid because Jesus is able to control the demons—if Jesus knows how they have dealt with the man, he might punish them for their uncaring ways. The pig herders and eyewitnesses seem to egg on the crowd, describing how the demons left the man, entering the pigs and driving them over the cliff. They have lost a great deal of money in this herd. Rather than feeling the joy of one man whose life is restored, they feel remorse and anger at all the profit they have lost. Rather than praising Jesus for the miracle, the crowd asks Jesus to leave them alone. Often people would rather have the dysfunction of their community than pay a price for significant change, even when someone benefits.

> ### Trivia Tidbit
>
> *The demons in the man said that their name was "Legion." According to scholar Adrian Goldsworthy, this was a Roman military group that varied in size over time but originally consisted of 4,200 foot soldiers and 300 soldiers on horseback.*

The man who was once possessed by demons has a different reaction: gratitude. Now freed of his affliction, he is told by Jesus to go out and tell his story to everyone for the glory of God. And where does the man go? Right back to the people who once chained him up! Jesus has so changed his life that he becomes a missionary to the very people who feared Jesus and sent him away. Because Jesus has cared for him, he turns and reaches out to those who need it most. He is able to express his love for the change Christ has brought to his life by attempting to love others and share the story of Christ's power with them. That is the power that God's graciousness can have in our lives as well.

Going Deeper Questions

3. What afflictions or struggles has God helped you with in your life? How have you thanked God for delivering you? Who have you shared this with lately?

_____

_____

_____

_____

_____

_____

4. If Jesus were to ask you directly to help those who have hurt you most, who would you go to and how would you reach out to them?

_____

_____

_____

_____

_____

_____

Today's Scripture

Luke 10:25-37; Romans 14

Key Verses

*"What is written in the law?" he replied. "How do you read it?"
He answered, "'Love the Lord your God with all your heart
and with all your soul and with all your strength and with all
your mind;' and, 'Love your neighbor as yourself.'"*

Luke 10:26-27 NIV

1. Write about a time when you acted like the priest or the Levite in this
   parable. Write about a time you acted like the Samaritan.

   _____

   _____

   _____

   _____

   _____

2. In each situation from the question above, what motivated you to act
   the way that you did?

   _____

   _____

   _____

   _____

   _____

Going Deeper

"Who is my neighbor?" It's a pretty simple question, but an important one. In this parable, the Samaritan is the best neighbor to the man injured on the road. Samaritans lived in the former southern kingdom of Israel, which had been overtaken by the Assyrians in 586 B.C. They had intermarried with the Assyrians and other tribes and had blended their religious practices with the religions of that area. For doing so, they were seen by most Jewish people as outsiders and blasphemers against God's order.

While it would have shocked the crowd that the hero of Jesus' story was a Samaritan, it would also have surprised them to see how he cared for the Jewish man. The priest and the Levite (a Jewish temple worker) had walked by the man, perhaps on their way to their God-given duties. If they interacted with blood or touched a man who was dead, they could not enter the temple unless they went through a lengthy ritual purification. They probably feared becoming ceremonially unclean and avoided the scene on that account.

> ## Trivia Tidbit
>
> *The Samaritan treated the hurt man's wounds with oil and wine. These items were not only dietary staples of the time, they were used in temple worship and were believed to have medicinal use as well.*

The Samaritan stopped and helped the man in both a physical and a spiritual way. He picked the man up and cleaned the man's wounds. He paid for the man's care. He planned to return, to continue caring for the man and perhaps to fellowship with him in his recovery. The Samaritan, who did not know the Jewish Law nearly to the degree of the lawyer or priest, fulfilled the Law completely regarding the love we are to show to others, especially those who are vulnerable and in need. In God's book, a neighbor isn't just something we are . . . it's something we should do.

Going Deeper Questions

3. Has anyone ever been a neighbor to you in a hard time? What did this person give up to help you through it?

_____

_____

_____

_____

_____

_____

_____

4. Who is your neighbor, and how can you help such a person using the blessings that God has given you?

_____

_____

_____

_____

_____

_____

_____

Day 4

Key Verse

We should all please our neighbors for their good, to build them up.

Romans 15:2 TNIV

1. What does Jesus teach about loving others in Luke 6?

_____

_____

_____

_____

_____

2. In Romans 15, what does Paul teach us about loving others in the church?

_____

_____

_____

_____

Going Deeper

This passage in Romans may seem a bit mean-spirited in the way that it categorizes Christians as either "weak" or "strong" in their faith. It can cause us to look at ourselves and think, "Well, am I a good enough Christian to be considered 'strong,' or am I one of the weak people that other good Christians have to help all the time?" One danger of this thinking is that, depending upon our answer, we can become either prideful in our supposed strength or self-loathing because of our assumed weakness. But that's not the purpose of this passage at all. It's not our job to judge ourselves . . . or others. Paul wants us to focus on our fellow Christians, not so that we can lump them into one category or another, but so that we recognize that *everyone* is weak sometimes. It is reminiscent of the chorus of the classic song "Lean on Me," where Bill Withers promises to be strong for his friend but points out that soon enough he'll need someone to lean on too.

> **Trivia Tidbit**
>
> *Most of the year, Israel is a dry place, but in late fall and early winter, winds from the Mediterranean blow in violent storms that cause flash flooding in the hard, dried stream beds.*

Everyone makes mistakes, and everyone has certain temptations and struggles that bother them more than others do. We need to be able to depend on our fellow Christians to help us in difficult times. The best way to do that is to work for the good of others and to build a loving community with others in the church. Paul reminds us that instead of focusing on whether *we* are weak or strong, we can encourage one another to understand and live out of Christ's will for each of us. Because, let's face it, all of us need someone to lean on sometimes, someone who can give us love and encouragement to keep the faith in all circumstances.

Going Deeper Questions

3. What do you find harder to stop: judging others or judging yourself? What do these passages teach you about each type of judging?

_____

_____

_____

_____

_____

_____

_____

4. What areas of weakness do you see in yourself? Who in your life can you trust to help you with these weaknesses?

_____

_____

_____

_____

_____

_____

_____

Today's Scripture

Isaiah 33; Galatians 5:1-6

Key Verse

For through the Spirit, by faith, we eagerly wait for the hope of righteousness.

Galatians 5:5 NRSV

1. List attributes and titles that are used in Isaiah 33 to describe God's character. What do these teach you about God's holiness?

_____

_____

_____

_____

_____

2. For Paul, what is the connection between freedom and love?

_____

_____

_____

_____

_____

Going Deeper

So, what was the deal with Paul and circumcision? Whenever he talks about it he seems to have a need for exclamation points. Paul preached that all people could be forgiven of their sins and have their lives turned around through faith in Jesus Christ. This was revolutionary for Paul. As a Pharisee he had spent a lifetime trying to free himself from sin and find forgiveness by keeping all of the Jewish Law and being faithful to the prescribed offerings and sacrifices made on his behalf at the Temple. One aspect of his obedience was the mark of circumcision that all male Jews shared.

> **Trivia Tidbit**
>
> *A yoke is a wooden beam placed across the shoulders or horns of large animals, particularly oxen, to control them and harness their power for some task, such as plowing a field or pulling a cart.*

This was a symbol of allegiance to the old covenant between God and the Hebrew people. In the Old Testament, circumcision was a sign of Israel's devotion to God. It was a physical sign that set them apart from other people in that time. It was required by law for all Jewish men.

The problem that Paul had with the Law of the Old Testament was that while it taught Israel how to live, it did not free them from sin. While it showed them what sacrifices to make for forgiveness, it never claimed their hearts with a desire for love of God through obedience to God. While circumcision set them apart, it also instilled a false confidence that said, in effect, "I'm special; I don't need to worry about my sin because I am already accepted by God as one of the circumcised."

When Paul accepted Jesus as the Christ and Messiah, he came to understand how Jesus' death on the cross was the perfect sacrifice for the sins of the world. Perhaps for the first time, Paul felt fully forgiven. Inspired by the love of Christ on the cross, Paul's heart changed: he longed to serve God not to simply avoid sin, but to be like Christ. Through faith in Christ, Paul accepted God's unmerited love. He came to have faith in the grace of Christ's love to transform lives, and in that grace alone.

When other Christians who also came from a Jewish background began telling converts to Christianity that they must first be circumcised, it angered Paul. He saw this requirement as a form of turning away from the new covenant in Christ and a return to making oneself righteous by keeping the old laws. Thus, circumcision did not represent a loving relationship with Christ or an acceptance of grace; it was a rejection of Christ as our sacrifice and an attempt to be favored based on our own strength. Paul knew something from personal experience: we're not strong enough to make it on our own. We need help from the Holy Spirit to stand strong in our struggles, and we receive that help by accepting Christ's ultimate sacrifice as our only hope. This is why Paul wrote in Galatians 5:6: "The only thing that counts is faith working through love."

Going Deeper Questions

3. How did Paul feel about the practice of circumcision? Why did it bother him?

_____

_____

_____

_____

_____

_____

_____

4. For Paul, what superseded the act of circumcision in the lives of Christians?

_____

_____

_____

_____

_____

_____

Notes

The following notes offer citations for the Trivia Tidbits found throughout this book. They are listed by week and day—for example, "4.1" means the Tidbit for week 4, day 1.

1.1—Andrew R. Fausset, "Leviathan," in *Fausset's Bible Dictionary* (1949), accessed February 4, 2014 (http://www.studylight.org/dic/fbd/view.cgi?n=2272).

1.2—Andrew R. Fausset, "East Wind," in *Fausset's Bible Dictionary* (1949), accessed February 4, 2014 (http://www.studylight.org/dic/fbd/view.cgi?n=1052).

1.3—"Star Survey Reaches 70 Sextillion," CNN (2003) accessed February 4, 2014 (http://www.cnn.com/2003/TECH/space/07/22/stars.survey/).

1.4—See Exodus 12:35-36; 32:2-4.

1.5—Andrew R. Fausset, "Shewbread," in *Fausset's Bible Dictionary* (1949), accessed February 4, 2014 (http://www.studylight.org/dic/fbd/view.cgi?n=3390).

2.1—*God's Game Plan: The Athletes' Bible,* Holman Christian Standard Version (Nashville: Holman Bible Publishers, 2005), pp. OT 171-172.

2.2—See Matthew 25:31-33, 41-46.

2.3—Among others, see Andrew R. Fausset, "Publican," in *Fausset's Bible Dictionary* (1949) (http://www.studylight.org/dic/fbd/view.cgi?n=3009); Louis Matthews Sweet, "Tax; Taxing," *International Standard Bible Encyclopedia*, ed. James Orr (Chicago: Howard-Severance, 1915), accessed February 4, 2014 (http://www.bible-history.com/isbe/T/TAX%3B+TAXING/).

2.4—Adrian Goldsworthy, *The Complete Roman Army* (London: Thames and Hudson, 2003), pp. 25, 215.

2.5—See Genesis 5:24 and 2 Kings 2:11; Mo Rocca, *All the Presidents' Pets* (New York: Crown, 2004), p. 38. The Presidential Pets Museum website has a fascinating list of furry White House denizens throughout the years (http://presidentialpetmuseum.com/whitehousepets-2/, accessed February 4, 2014).

3.1—"Levi," in *Jewish Encyclopedia* (New York: Funk and Wagnalls, 1901–1906), accessed February 7, 2014 (http://www.jewishencyclopedia.com/articles/9800-levi); Andrew Wommack, "Notes on John 5:1," accessed February 7, 2014 (http://www.awmi.net/bible/joh_05_01).

3.2—Plato, *The Republic*, trans. Benjamin Jowett (New York: The Modern Library, 1941); "Epistle to the Hebrews," *Catholic Encyclopedia*, accessed February 7, 2014 (https://www.catholic.org/encyclopedia/view.php?id=5596).

3.3—"Sanitation in Ancient Rome," accessed February 15, 2014 (http://en.wikipedia.org/wiki/Sanitation_in_ancient_Rome).

3.4—*God's Game Plan: The Athletes' Bible*, p. NT 338.

3.5—Jewish Life Foundation, "History of the Maccabiah Games," accessed February 7, 2014 (http://www.jewishlifefoundation.org/Maccabiah.History.pdf).

4.1—See Genesis 11.

4.2—See Exodus 19; 1 Kings 19; Deuteronomy 34; Genesis 22.

4.3—Donald B. DeYoung, *Weather and the Bible: 100 Questions and Answers* (Grand Rapids, Mich.: Baker Books, 1992), p. 66.

4.4—W. Ewing, "Bethsaida," *International Standard Bible Encyclopedia,* ed. James Orr (Chicago: Howard-Severance, 1915), accessed February 15, 2014 (http://www.bible-history.com/isbe/B/BETHSAIDA/).

4.5—See Exodus 3; 13; 20.

5.1—*God's Game Plan: The Athletes' Bible,* p. NT 110.

5.2—See 1 Kings 16:30; 22:38 NIV.

5.3—George V. Wigram, *The Englishman's Greek Concordance of the New Testament* (1st ed. 1840; Peabody, Mass.: Hendrickson Publishers, 1996), citing Matthew 26:25, Mark 9:5, and John 3:2 (among others); Luke 12:13.

5.4—Barton W. Johnson, "Matthew Chapter XII," in *People's New Testament,* accessed February 7, 2014 (http://www.biblestudytools.com/commentaries/peoples-new-testament/matthew/12.html).

5.5—William Barclay, *The Parables of Jesus* (Louisville, Ky.: Westminster John Knox Press, 1999), pp. 92-98.

6.1—*God's Game Plan: The Athletes' Bible*, pp. NT 409, NT 445; Jonah 2:2; Job 7:9.

6.2—Goldsworthy, *The Complete Roman Army*, pp. 27, 28.

6.3—See Exodus 29:40; 1 Timothy 5:23.

6.4—*God's Game Plan: The Athletes' Bible,* p. NT 87.

6.5—"Yoke," *Merriam-Webster Dictionary*, accessed February 7, 2014 (http://www.merriam-webster.com/dictionary/yoke).